A Note to Parents

DK READERS is a compelling program for beginning readers, designed in conjunction with leading literacy experts, including Dr. Linda Gambrell, Distinguished Professor of Education at Clemson University. Dr. Gambrell has served as President of the National Reading Conference, the College Reading Association, and the International Reading Association.

Beautiful illustrations and superb full-color photographs combine with engaging, easy-to-read stories to offer a fresh approach to each subject in the series. Each DK READER is guaranteed to capture a child's interest while developing his or her reading skills, general knowledge, and love of reading.

The five levels of DK READERS are aimed at different reading abilities, enabling you to choose the books that are exactly right for your child:

Pre-level 1: Learning to read
Level 1: Beginning to read
Level 2: Beginning to read alone
Level 3: Reading alone
Level 4: Proficient readers

The "normal" age at which a child begins to read can be anywhere from three to eight years old. Adult participation through the lower levels is very helpful for providing encouragement, discussing storylines, and sounding out unfamiliar words.

No matter which level you select, you can be sure that you are helping your child learn to read, then read to learn!

LONDON, NEW YORK, MUNICH,
MELBOURNE, AND DELHI

Editor Shari Last
Managing Editor Laura Gilbert
Managing Art Editor Maxine Pedliham
Art Director Lisa Lanzarini
Publishing Manager Julie Ferris
Publishing Director Simon Beecroft
Pre-Production Producer Siu Yin Chan

DK India
Assistant Editor Gaurav Joshi
Senior Editor Garima Sharma
Art Editor Anamica Roy, Divya Jain
Deputy Managing Art Editor Neha Ahuja
Pre-Production Manager Sunil Sharma

Reading Consultant
Linda B. Gambrell, Ph.D.

For Lucasfilm
Executive Editor J. W. Rinzler
Art Director Troy Alders
Keeper of the Holocron Leland Chee
Director of Publishing Carol Roeder

First American Edition, 2014
10 9 8 7 6 5 4 3
003-187418-Mar/14

Published in the United States by DK Publishing
345 Hudson Street, New York, New York 10014

Published in Great Britain by Dorling Kindersley Limited

A catalog record for this book is available
from the Library of Congress.

ISBN: 978-1-4654-1680-3 (Paperback)
ISBN: 978-1-4654-1681-0 (Hardcover)

Color reproduction by Alta Image Ltd., UK
Printed and bound in the U.S.A. by Lake Book Manufacturing, Inc.

Discover more at
www.dk.com
www.starwars.com

DK READERS

LEARNING TO READ
pre-level 1

STAR WARS

Can you spot a
Jedi?

Written by Shari Last

Who is this Jedi?

Is it Luke Skywalker, Plo Koon, or Yoda?

It is Yoda.

Jedi

Yoda is a
small, green
Jedi Master.

Look at all that
shiny metal!

Is this a
clone trooper
or a droid?

Droid

It is a droid
named C-3PO.

C-3PO is
built from
wires and
metal.

Look at this yellow
and gray starship!

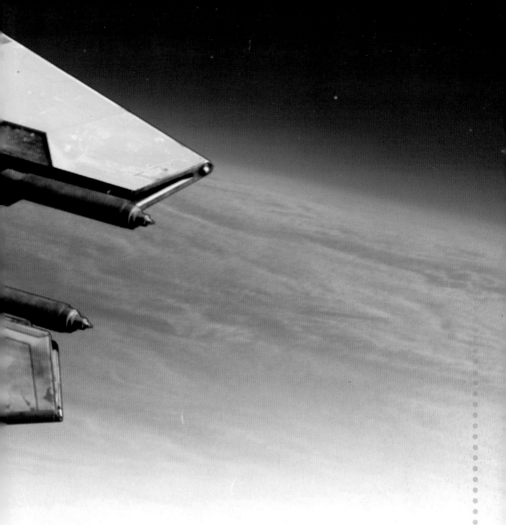

Does it belong to
Anakin, Obi-Wan,
or Mace Windu?

It belongs to
Anakin Skywalker.

Starship

He is a famous Jedi pilot.

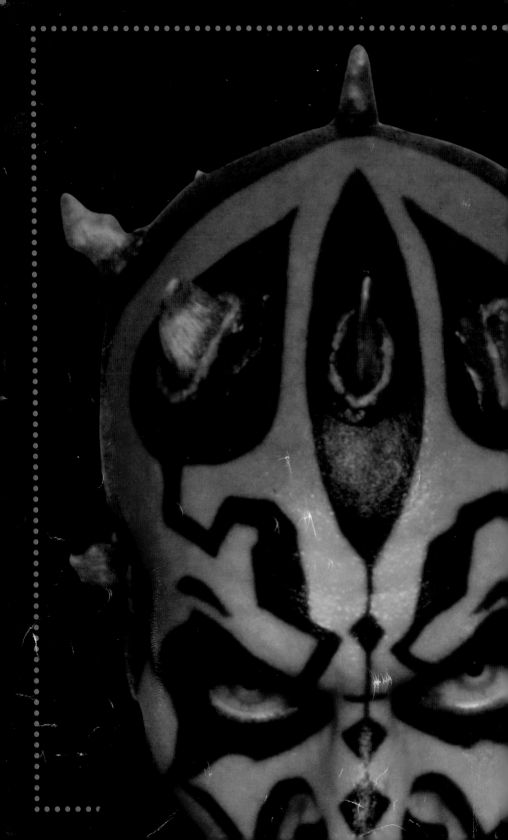

Look at all
those horns!

Is it Mace Windu,
Darth Maul,
or Chewbacca?

Darth Maul

It is Darth Maul.

He has a red and
black painted face.

What a funny creature!

Is it R2-D2,
Obi-Wan Kenobi,
or Jar Jar Binks?

It is
Jar Jar Binks.

Jar Jar Binks

Jar Jar is a Gungan
from the planet
of Naboo.

Who is this
hairy creature?

Is it an Ewok,
a Wookiee,
or a Jawa?

It is a Wookiee.

Wookiee

Wookiees are very
tall and very strong.

Now you have discovered these creatures and vehicles.

What will you spot next?

Wookiee

Yoda

Starship

Jar Jar Binks

Darth Maul

C-3PO

Glossary

Droid
A type of robot.

Gungan
Someone who lives underwater on Naboo.

Jedi
Someone who protects the galaxy.

Metal
A shiny, hard material.

Starship
A ship that travels through outer space.

Index

Here are some other DK Readers you might enjoy.

Pre-Level 1

Star Wars: Even Droids Need Friends
Discover the unusual friendships that can form
in the *Star Wars* galaxy.

Star Wars: The Clone Wars: Masters of the Force
Meet the Jedi and the Sith, and learn about their
amazing powers as true Masters of the Force.

**Star Wars: The Clone Wars:
Don't Wake the Zillo Beast!**
Meet the fearsome Zillo Beast, and learn about lots of
other strange *Star Wars* creatures.

Level 1

Star Wars: Are Ewoks Scared of Stormtroopers?
Meet the bravest heroes in the *Star Wars* galaxy,
who defeat evil villains against all odds.

Star Wars: The Clone Wars: Ahsoka in Action!
Learn all about Padawan Ahsoka Tano's combat skills,
as she battles her enemies in the Clone Wars.